Jokes for Children

JOKES
for
CHILDREN

by

MARGUERITE KOHL
FREDERICA YOUNG

Illustrated by Bob Patterson

HILL AND WANG · NEW YORK
A division of Farrar, Straus and Giroux

Quality Printing and Binding by:
R.R. Donnelley & Sons Company
1009 Sloan Street
Crawfordsville, IN 47933 U.S.A.

Manufactured in the United States of America

0-374-43832-3

Foreword

The most important thing you should know about this book is that it was written to fill a need. The list of joke books for children is very limited and the few books that exist are in great demand.

Humor—especially in children—is a very personal reaction. Listen to a child tell a joke to members of his own age group. Chances are it will make one child rock with laughter, cause the second to double up, and bring only a mild giggle from the third. The last child may not understand the joke—but he does want to laugh.

This book is designed to give many children an opportunity to laugh. We can't pretend there was anything scientific about assembling our collection, but there was something very personal—a child's reaction to each joke. We have included jokes children told us, told their parents, told each other. We have also included jokes they selected for their school publications and theatrical productions.

It was our good fortune to be able to use the large cast of a children's community show as an "advisory panel." The children reviewed the jokes and selected those they wanted to tell on stage.

The book is divided into sections or categories, only because that seems to be the way jokes are recalled and related. When one child tells a joke involving school, this brings on another and another—all school oriented. The same practice is repeated with family, animals, riddles, and the other groups. And there are cases where children have adapted a joke to fit several categories and can't seem to decide which is their favorite. In such instances we have included more than one version of the same joke.

MARGUERITE KOHL and FREDERICA YOUNG

October, 1963

Contents

Contents

Jokes for Children

Teachers and Pupils

FIRST STUDENT: How were your exam questions?
SECOND STUDENT: They were easy, but I had trouble with
the answers.

TEACHER: What is your favorite state, Sam?
SAM: Mississippi.
TEACHER: How do you spell it?
SAM: Er . . . I like Ohio much better.

FIRST SCHOOL FRIEND: She told me that you told her the
secret I told you not to tell her.
SECOND SCHOOL FRIEND: But I told her not to tell you
I told her!
FIRST SCHOOL FRIEND: Oh, well, don't tell her I told you
that she told me.

A teacher asked her first-grade class to bring their birth certificates to class. When the time came to give them to her, David stood up and said very politely, "Teacher, I forgot my excuse for being born."

PRINCIPAL: This is the fourth time you have been to my office this week. What have you to say for yourself, Christopher?
CHRISTOPHER: I'm certainly glad that today is Friday.

AUNTY: How did Jennifer do on her history exam?
MOTHER: Not very well. But it wasn't her fault. They asked her about things that happened before she was born.

STEVIE: Hey, Mom, I got a hundred in school today.
MOM: That's wonderful! What did you get a hundred in?
STEVIE: In two things: I got forty in reading and sixty in spelling.

STUDENT: But I don't think I deserve a zero on this exam.
TEACHER: Neither do I, but it's the lowest mark I can give you.

TEACHER: You can be sure that if Shakespeare were alive today, he'd be considered a remarkable man.
LEROY: He sure ought to be, he'd be more than three hundred years old!

TEACHER: Is there anything you can do better than anyone else?
PEGGY: Yes, sir, read my own handwriting.

TEACHER: What do you call the last teeth we get?
MICHAEL: False teeth.

TEACHER: Tell me the truth now, who did your homework?
WALLIE: Dad.
TEACHER: All alone?
WALLIE: No, I helped him with it.

HUBIE: Teacher, would you scold anybody for something they didn't do?
TEACHER: Of course not, why?
HUBIE: Well, I didn't do my arithmetic.

FIRST STUDENT: I'm taking French, Spanish, and Algebra this year.
SECOND STUDENT: O.K.—let me hear you say "good evening" in Algebra.

SMARTY: How many books can you put into an empty school bag?
FRIEND: I don't know, how many?
SMARTY: One—because after that is in, the bag won't be empty.

TEACHER: Why do you keep scratching yourself, Mary?
MARY: I'm the only one who knows where it itches.

TEACHER: How do you spell "inconsequentially"?
BILLIE: Wrong.

TEACHER: Give me an example of a collective noun.
JIMMY: A magnet.

TEACHER (angrily): You should have been here at nine!
SANDY: Why? What happened?

TEACHER: How would you punctuate the following sentence: "I saw a five-dollar bill on the street."
GREG: I'd make a dash after it.

The kindergarten teacher struggled to put on each child's boots after a long rainy morning. It had taken her a while to get Martin's on when he said: "These aren't mine."

The tired teacher took them off and asked: "Whose are they?"

Martin replied: "They're my brother's, but my mother lets me wear them."

TEACHER: What comes after O?
DOPEY: Yeah.

TEACHER: Tony, use these words in a sentence—*defense, detail, deduct, defeat.*

TONY: De-feat of de-duct went over de-fense before de-tail.

TEACHER: Why are you late, Eddie?

EDDIE: Well, a sign down the road said . . .

TEACHER: Now, what can a sign possibly have to do with this?

EDDIE: The sign says, School ahead, go slow.

TEACHER: Why is it, Freddie, that everyone else had a five-page report on milk and your composition is only a half-page?

FREDDIE: I was writing about condensed milk.

A teacher wrote on one of his student's report cards: "David is a good student, but he talks too much."

David's father signed and returned the report card with this comment: "You should meet his mother."

TEACHER: Come up here and give me whatever you have in your mouth.

JEFF: I wish I could. It's a toothache.

TEACHER: Can anyone here tell me some of the uses of cowhide?

BARBARA: Well, it helps keep the cow together.

TEACHER: If we breathe oxygen in the daytime, what do we breathe at night?
JONAS: Nitrogen.

HOMEMAKING TEACHER: And now girls, for your final examination—eat what you have made.

A little boy had heard about how crowded the schools were in his city and was discussing the problem with his grade-school principal. After listening to the little fellow for a few minutes, the principal said to him, "I think it's very thoughtful of you, but I don't really feel that your resignation is the solution to our crowded school problem."

TEACHER: Johnny, name two pronouns.
JOHNNY: Who, me?
TEACHER: That's correct.

TEACHER: Beatrice, can you tell me where the Red Sea is?
BEATRICE: Yes, ma'am, it's on the third line of my report card.

TEACHER: If I laid two eggs on this side of the table and two eggs on that side of the table, how many would I have?

GRETCHEN: I don't know, teacher, but I bet you couldn't do it.

TEACHER: Bobby, if you put your hand in one pants pocket and found seventy-five cents and you put your hand in the other pants pocket and found twenty-five cents, what would you have?

BOBBY: I'd have somebody else's pants on.

TEACHER: As we walk outdoors on a cold winter morning and look around us, what do we see on every hand?

FIRST-GRADER: Gloves!

TEACHER: Yes, Tommy, what is it?

TOMMY: I don't want to scare you, but Pop said if I didn't get better grades, someone is due for a licking.

The teacher spent the period reading to her class about the rhinoceros family. When she finished, she said, "Name some things that are very dangerous to get near to and have horns."

Junior spoke up without hesitation: "Automobiles."

TEACHER: If I gave you two apples and told you to give one to your brother, would you give him the little one or the big one?

TEDDIE: Do you mean my little brother or my big brother?

TEACHER: If you have fourteen potatoes and must divide them equally among seven persons, how would you do it?

HARRY: I'd mash them.

TEACHER: Catherine, what would you do if a man-eating tiger were chasing you?

CATHERINE: Nothing, 'cause I'm a girl.

The teacher wrote on the blackboard: "I ain't had no fun all summer." Then she asked a youngster in the front row: "Harry, what should I do to correct that?"

Harry answered: "Get a boy friend, maybe?"

BOY IN GEOGRAPHY CLASS: "The principal export of the United States is money."

TEACHER: You're the laziest boy I've ever known. Aren't you quick at something?

DANNY: Yes, sir, nobody can get tired as quickly as I can.

TEACHER: What was the most wonderful accomplishment of the Romans?

ARTHUR: Learning Latin.

TEACHER: Why were the Dark Ages so called?

GENEVIEVE: Because they had so many knights.

A girl in the senior class was wearing a brand new ring, but no one noticed it. At lunch in the cafeteria she said suddenly: "My it's hot in here! I think I'll take off my ring."

TEACHER: Why were you late for school?
BELINDA: There are eight people in our family, and the alarm was set for seven.

JUNIOR: I'm not going to school any more.
MOTHER: Why not?
JUNIOR: On Monday the teacher said four and four make eight.
On Tuesday she said six and two make eight.
Today she said seven and one are eight.
So I'm not going back to school till she makes up her mind.

FATHER: How are your grades, son?
SON: Under water, Dad.
FATHER: Under water, what do you mean?
SON: They're below C level.

A conceited high-school student was bragging about his abilities to the store manager while looking for a summer job. Finally he said, "Surely you have an opening for someone like me?"

"Yes, I do," answered the manager, "and please close it gently as you go out."

TEACHER: Timmy, how many sexes are there?
TIMMY: Three.
TEACHER: What? Name them.
TIMMY: Female sex, male sex, and insex.

MOTHER: I'm a little worried about your being at the foot of the class.
SONNY: Don't worry about that. They teach the same stuff at both ends.

ENGLISH TEACHER: Now tell me, what is the opposite of the word "misery"?
CLASS: Happiness.
TEACHER: And sadness?
CLASS: Gladness.
TEACHER: And the opposite of "woe"?
CLASS: Giddap.

TEACHER: What is the difference between electricity and lightning?
PUPIL: We don't have to pay for lightning.

TEACHER: Before we begin this final exam, are there any questions?
STUDENT: What's the name of this course?

TEACHER: What is the main use of our skin?
BILLY: It makes us look more natural.

AUNTIE: Well, Petie, how do you like school?
PETIE: Closed!

TEACHER: What do hippopotamuses have that no other
animals have?
LOUIE: Little hippopotamuses.

SUNDAY-SCHOOL TEACHER: Who was Peter?
LITTLE BOY: I think he was a wabbit.

HOPEFUL MOTHER: Is my son really trying?
TEACHER: Very!

TEACHER: Bob, give me a sentence using "officiate."
BOB: A man got sick from a-fish-he-ate.

EXAM QUESTION: What's the best way to prevent infec-
tion caused by biting insects?
DOPEY'S ANSWER: Don't bite any.

A problem child was brought to the principal's office.

PRINCIPAL: Do you ever do your homework?

FRESH KID: Oh, now and then.

PRINCIPAL: Where do you do it?

FRESH KID: Oh, here and there.

PRINCIPAL: Put him in that closet.

FRESH KID: Hey! When will I get out?

PRINCIPAL: Oh, sooner or later.

TEACHER: You missed school yesterday, didn't you?

SALLY: Not a bit.

DICK: Hurray! The teacher said we'd have a test today, rain or shine.

HARRY: What's so good about that?

DICK: It's snowing.

MOTHER'S FRIEND: Do you go to school?

LITTLE BOY: No, ma'am, I'm sent.

TEACHER: Muriel, I hope I didn't see you looking at Jenny's paper.

MURIEL: I hope you didn't either!

TEACHER: What is an Indian woman called, Buddy?

BUDDY: A squaw.

TEACHER: And what is an Indian baby called?

BUDDY: A squawker.

JOHNNY (arriving home with his report card): I was the highest of all who failed.

TEACHER: Where does steel wool come from?
JUNIOR: Er . . . from the sheep that live in the Iron Mountains.

MISS TEACH (telling beginner's story): I am round. I often keep my head in my house. I move very slowly. Who am I?
FIRST-GRADER: You are Miss Teach.

PUPIL: What did I make in arithmetic?
TEACHER: Mistakes!

TEACHER: What is water, Bobby?
BOBBY: It's a colorless liquid that turns black when I put my hands in it.

TEACHER: But where is the dot over the *i*?
STUDENT: It's still in the pencil.

TEACHER: Where is your pencil, Jeff?
JEFF: I ain't got one.
TEACHER: Don't say *ain't*. Listen: I don't have a pencil. You don't have a pencil. They don't have a pencil.
JEFF: Gee, where did all the pencils go?

TEACHER: There are two words I never allow my pupils to use. One is *swell* and the other is *lousy*.
BOY: And what are the words?

TEACHER: How's your typing speed coming along?
MARY: Fine, I can do thirty mistakes a minute.

TEACHER: Order, children, order!
PUPIL: I'll have cake and ice cream.

TEACHER: If your mother had ten dollars and your father took two dollars, what would your mother have?
TEDDY: A fit!

TEACHER: Dottie, what wouldn't we have if cave men had not discovered fire?
DOTTIE: Chimneys.

TEACHER: Why the horseshoe, Dick?
DICK: For luck—I'm scared of exams.
TEACHER: But we don't have an exam today.
DICK: See, it's helping already.

TEACHER: Joan, how are you doing with your arithmetic?
JOAN: Well, I've learned to add the zeros, but the figures still bother me.

TEACHER: This composition on "Our Dog" is exactly the same as your sister's.

BENNY: Yes, ma'am, it's the same dog.

TEACHER: Name five things that contain milk.

DUSTY: Butter, cheese, ice cream, and . . . and . . . two cows.

TEACHER: Rudy, tell me where the elephant is found.

RUDY: An elephant is too big to get lost.

Melissa

MOTHER: What are you looking for, Melissa?
MELISSA: Nothing.
MOTHER: You'll find it in the box where the candy was.

MOTHER: Come in, Missy, and I'll give you something to eat. Are your feet dirty?
MISSY: Yes, Mother, but I've got my shoes on.

Melissa disobeyed her mother so was sent for a switch to be punished with. She was gone for quite a while and when she finally came back her mother asked her for the switch. Melissa cried and said, "The tree was too big for me to reach, but here's a rock you can throw at me."

MELISSA: Mom, do you remember that vase you always worried I would break?

MOTHER: Yes, what about it?

MELISSA: Your worries are over.

UNCLE: If you're really good, Melissa, I'll give you this bright new penny.

MELISSA: Haven't you got a dirty old quarter?

MELISSA: Grandma, can you eat nuts?

GRANDMA: No, dear, they don't agree with me.

MELISSA: O.K.—then you can mind my peanuts till I come home from school.

FATHER: Well, Melissa, how do you like your new baby brother?

MELISSA: Oh, I guess he's all right, but there are lots of things we needed worse.

VISITOR: And what will you do, dear, when you are as big as your mother?

MELISSA: Diet.

FATHER: Is that a cat you're painting?

MELISSA: Yes.

FATHER: Where's the tail?

MELISSA: It's still in the paint box.

FATHER: Stop reaching, haven't you got a tongue?
MELISSA: Yes, but my arms are longer.

Mother is wiping Melissa's tears.
MELISSA: It's no use, I'm not finished crying yet.

AUNTIE: Melissa, you must have grown another foot since I last saw you.
MELISSA: No, I still have only two.

MELISSA: Mother, when I get old, will my head be bare-footed like Grandpa's?

MOTHER: Now, Melissa, you must not be selfish. You must let your brother have the sled half the time.
MELISSA: But Mother, I do. I have it going down the hill, and he has it coming up.

MOTHER: I wish you'd run across the street and see how old Mrs. Jones is.

MELISSA: I've already been, and Mrs. Jones says it's none of my business how old she is.

SUNDAY-SCHOOL TEACHER: Can any of you children tell me who lived in the Garden of Eden?

MELISSA: Yes, teacher, I think it was the Adamses.

FATHER: Melissa, why don't you wash your face? I can see what you had for breakfast this morning.

MELISSA: What was it?

FATHER: Eggs.

MELISSA: Wrong, Pop, that was yesterday.

Melissa was told to go hide herself in her mother's closet until she could behave herself. After a long silence her mother went to the door and asked, "Now do you want to come out and behave yourself?"

Melissa answered, "Not yet, I spit on your shoes, I spit on your dresses, I spit on your hats and now I'm waiting for more spit."

MOTHER: There were two pieces of pie in the kitchen this morning. Now there is only one. Can you explain this, Melissa?

MELISSA: Yes, it was so dark, I couldn't see the other piece.

OLDER GIRL: Have you lived here all your life?
MELISSA: Not yet.

MOTHER: Your hair needs cutting badly.
MELISSA: I think it needs cutting nicely, it was cut badly last time.

MOTHER: Melissa, be sure to wash your arms before you put on that clean blouse.
MELISSA: For long or short sleeves?

MOTHER: Why did you put this frog in your little brother's bed?
MELISSA: Because I couldn't find a mouse.

MOTHER: What on earth is in the oven?
MELISSA: I dropped one of your candles in the dishwater, so I put it in the oven to dry.

MOTHER: Melissa, how did I happen to catch you with your hand in the cookie jar?
MELISSA: I guess it's because I didn't hear you coming.

FRIEND: What does the word "spunk" mean?
MELISSA: Well, after your father spanks you, you're spunk.

MELISSA: Mother, look at that man! He doesn't have any hair at all.

MOTHER: Shhhh, he might hear you.

MELISSA: Doesn't he know it?

MELISSA: Mommy, the boy next door broke my dolly.

MOMMY: That's too bad, dear, how did he do it?

MELISSA: I hit him over the head with it.

MELISSA: Mother, I can't thread this needle.

MOTHER: Why not?

MELISSA: It keeps shutting its eye.

MELISSA: Did you know we are related?

FRIEND: Goodness, no.

MELISSA: Yes, we are. Your dog is my dog's brother.

MOTHER: Oh-oh, I forgot to shake this medicine before I gave it to you.

MELISSA: That's all right, I'll just turn a few handsprings.

AUNT: What do you want to be when you grow up?
MELISSA: I'm going to join a circus and be a midget.
AUNT: You're too big for a midget.
MELISSA: That's the idea, I'll be the biggest midget in the world.

MELISSA: Our new next-door neighbors must be very poor.
MOTHER: What makes you say that?
MELISSA: You should have heard the russ they made when their baby swallowed a penny.

DOCTOR: Now, Melissa, stick out your tongue.
MELISSA: Nothing doing, I got in trouble for doing that at home.

GRANDMA: Were you a good girl at church today, Melissa?
MELISSA: I certainly was. A nice man offered me a whole plate full of money, and I said, No, thank you.

MELISSA: Mommy, is *water works* two words, or is there a hydrant in between?

MOTHER: Now, Melissa, don't you know you are not supposed to eat with your knife?
MELISSA: Yes, Mother, but my fork leaks.

MOTHER: What do you want to take cod-liver oil with
    today?
MELISSA: A fork.

MOTHER: Aunt Maud will never kiss you good-by if you
    have such a dirty face.
MELISSA: That's what I thought.

Rhymes

History is a dreadful subject
As dead as dead can be.
Once it killed the Romans
And now it's killing me.

Hickory dickory dock,
The mice ran up the clock.
The clock struck one,
And the others escaped with minor injuries.

Roses are red
Violets are blue
I love me—why don't you?

Kathy had a little car
And it was painted red.
And everywhere that Kathy went,
The cops picked up the dead.

Mary had a little lamb
And tied him to a heater.
And everytime he turned around,
He burned his little seater.

I had written to Aunt Maud,
Who was on a trip abroad,
When I heard she'd died of cramp
Just too late to save the stamp.

As I was standing in the street,
As quiet as could be,
A great big ugly man came up
And tied his horse to me.

I always eat peas with honey,
I've done it all my life,
They do taste kind of funny,
But it keeps them on the knife.

I love to stand upon my head and think great thoughts
        sublime,
Until my mother interrupts and says, "It's dinnertime."

The study of English for me,
Is a constant struggle, you see.
The teacher's all right,
If we don't have a fight—
But I'm glad when it's twenty past three.

In the family drinking well
Willie pushed his sister Nell.
She's there yet, because it kilt her—
Now we have to buy a filter.

Willie, with a thirst for gore,
Nailed his sister to the door.
Mother said, with humor quaint:
"Now, Willie dear, don't scratch the paint."

I got a dog, his name is Rover.
He's fluffy and soft and brown all over.
He's as cute and cuddly as sugar babies.
It's sure too bad that he's got rabies.

Little Willie shot his sister;
She was dead before we missed her.
Willie's always up to tricks.
Ain't he cute? He's only six.

Said the toe to the sock: "Let me through, let me through."
Said the sock to the toe: "I'll be darned if I do."

Four and twenty blackbirds
Baked in a pie.
When the pie was opened,
The birds began to sing,
"I love you truly."

Mary had a little lamb,
Its fleece was white as snow;
And everywhere that Mary went,
She took a bus.

Algy met a bear,
The bear was bulgy,
The bulge was Algy.

There once was a young circus dancer,
Who tugged at the tail of her prancer.
People shouted, "You fool,
That horse is a mule."
But they never received any answer.

I shot an arrow into the air
It fell to earth I know not where.
I lose more darn arrows that way.

Little Jack Horner, sat in a corner,
Eating his pumpkin pie.
He put in his thumb, pulled out a plum,
And said, "Well, I'll be doggoned."

Mary, Mary, quite contrary,
How does your garden grow?
With silver bells and cockle shells
And one pale pink petunia.

Mary had a little lamb,
Its fleece was white as snow;
She put it on the mantlepiece,
And now look at the doggone thing.

Humpty Dumpty sat on a wall,
Humpty Dumpty had a great fall;
All the King's horses and all the King's men
Had scrambled eggs.

Little Miss Muffet sat on a tuffet,
Eating her curds and whey;
Along came a spider, who sat down beside her,
And said, "Is this seat taken?"

A tutor who tooted a flute,
Tried to teach two young tooters to toot.
Said the two to the tutor,
Is it harder to toot,
Or to tutor two tooters to toot?

A flea and a fly in a flue were caught,
So what could they do?
Said the fly, Let us flee
Let us fly, said the flea.
So they flew through a flaw in the flue.

Fatty and Skinny went to bed.
Fatty rolled over and
Skinny was dead.

Star light, star bright,
First star I see tonight,
I wish I may, I wish I might . . .
Oh, nuts, it's a satellite!

Gruesomes

Why do they put a fence around the graveyard?
Because so many people are dying to get in.

MAN PASSING A CEMETERY: Do you know how many
   dead people there are in that cemetery?
SECOND MAN: All of them.

PROSECUTOR: Now tell the jury the truth, please. Why did
   you shoot your husband with a bow and arrow?
DEFENDANT: I didn't want to wake the children.

LITTLE BOY: I've just swallowed a great big worm.
FRIEND: Hadn't you better take something for it?
LITTLE BOY: No, I'll let it starve.

A farmer was driving his truck past a mental institution. An inmate asked him what he was hauling, and he said, "Fortilizer."

INMATE: What are you going to do with it?

FARMER: Put it on my strawberries.

INMATE: You should be here, not me; we put sugar and cream on them here.

EXECUTIONER: Have you any last words?

PRISONER: Yes, this will be a lesson to me.

FIRST CANNIBAL: Am I late for chow?

SECOND CANNIBAL: Yes, everybody's eaten.

NEIGHBOR: I think your son is spoiled.

FATHER: I completely disagree with you.

NEIGHBOR: Well, come out and see what a steam roller just did to him.

FRIST LADY: What has twenty-four feet, green eyes, and a pink body with purple stripes around it?

SECOND LADY: I don't know—what?

FIRST LADY: I don't know either, but you'd better pick it off your neck!

CUSTOMER: Say, what's this in my soup?

WAITER: I can't say, sir, I don't know one insect from another.

A grave digger, thinking of a fight he had just had with his wife, dug so deeply that he discovered he was down so far he couldn't climb out. When night fell he called out for help when he heard someone nearby. The passer-by looked down and saw him, so the grave digger was relieved and said, "Help me out, please, it's cold down here." The passer-by looked surprised for a minute, and then started shoveling dirt into the hole, saying, "No wonder you're cold, there's no dirt on you."

MISSIONARY: Why are you looking at me that way?
CANNIBAL: I am a food inspector.

Mommy! The power mower just cut off my foot.
Stay outside till it stops bleeding, dear, I just mopped.

MOTHER: How did you get along with your father while I was away?
SON: Just fine. Every morning he took me down to the lake in the boat and let me swim back.
MOTHER: My, that's a long swim, isn't it?
SON: I made it all right. The only trouble I had was getting out of the bag.

LITTLE BOY TO NEIGHBOR: If you give us a quarter, my little brother will imitate a hen.
NEIGHBOR: What will he do, cackle?
LITTLE BOY: He wouldn't do a silly imitation like that, he'll eat a worm.

What has four wheels and flies?
A garbage truck.

One day a man was riding through a deserted prairie. He came to a village and found there had been a massacre. Only one man was alive, and he had a big dagger in his chest. His rescuer went to help him and asked, "Does it hurt?"

The man replied, "Only when I laugh."

What is worse than finding a worm in an apple?
Finding only half a worm.

Two kids were looking out a window on a rainy day. A funeral procession went by, and one kid turned to the other and said, "Who's dead?"

The other kid replied, "The person in the first car behind the flowers."

MOTHER CANNIBAL TO WITCH DOCTOR: I'm worried about Junior, he wants to be a vegetarian.

Two men met in a restaurant.

FIRST MAN: I have a wife who is a millionairess.

SECOND MAN: That's good.

FIRST MAN: No, that isn't so good. She doesn't give me a penny of it.

SECOND MAN: That's too bad.

FIRST MAN: No, it isn't too bad, she's got a fifty-room mansion.

SECOND MAN: That's good.

FIRST MAN: No, it isn't so good.

SECOND MAN: Why?

FIRST MAN: It burned down one day.

SECOND MAN: Oh, that's bad.

FIRST MAN: No, it isn't so bad. My wife was in it.

Have you heard about the bop cannibal who ate three squares a day?

What would a cannibal be who ate his mother's sister?
I'll bite, what?
An aunt-eater, of course.

A witch doctor asked a cannibal what he had eaten lately to cause his stomach trouble. The cannibal said he had eaten a bald man, dressed in a brown tunic with a rope tied around his middle and wearing sandals. The witch doctor asked how he had cooked him, and the cannibal answered that he boiled him.

"No wonder," said the witch doctor, "he was a friar."

DRIVER: Must be getting close to town—we're hitting more people.

Sunday-school pupil looking at a picture of the early Christians being fed to the lions: "Gee, look at that poor little lion in the back. He won't get any!"

The foreman of a lumber camp put one of his new men to work at a circular saw. As he walked away he heard the man say, "Ouch."
FOREMAN: What happened?
WORKMAN: Dunno, I just stuck out my hand like this and—well, I'll be darned, there goes another one!

SURGEON SEWING UP PATIENT: "That's enough out of you."

LITTLE GIRL CANNIBAL: Mommy, is that airplane up there good to eat?
MOTHER CANNIBAL: Just like a lobster—only what's inside.

MOTHER CANNIBAL TO CHILD: How many times have I
told you not to speak with someone in your mouth?

There was the man who died from drinking varnish. It
was an awful sight but a beautiful finish.

PILOT CALLING TOWER: We're out of gas three hundred
miles over the Atlantic. What shall I do?
TOWER TO PILOT: Repeat after me—Our Father who art
in heaven . . .

PATIENT: Doctor what can I do about these little green
men crawling all over me?
DOCTOR: Just don't brush any on me.

WIFE: Doctor, come quickly. My husband has swallowed
a fountain pen.
DOCTOR: I'll be right over. What are you doing in the
meantime?
WIFE: I'm using a pencil.

FATHER: Broke my kid of biting his nails.
FRIEND: You did—how?
FATHER: Knocked his teeth out.

PROFESSOR AS HIS GLASS EYE ROLLED DOWN THE DRAIN: I
guess I've lost another pupil.

CHAPLAIN TO CONDEMNED MAN IN ELECTRIC CHAIR: Anything I can do for you?
PRISONER: Yeah, hold my hand.

CANNIBAL CHIEF TO VICTIM: What did you do for a living?
VICTIM: I was an associate editor.
CHIEF: Cheer up, after tonight you'll be editor-in-chief.

EXPLORER TO EDUCATED CANNIBAL: Do you mean to say that you went to a university and you still eat your enemies?
CANNIBAL: Yes, but of course now I use a knife and fork.

Riddles

What is the difference between a bottle of medicine and a naughty boy?
One is well shaken before taken, the other is taken and well shaken.

Why did the little boy put his car on the stove?
He wanted a hot rod.

Why is a farmer famous?
Because he's outstanding in his field.

What state is round at the ends and high in the middle?
O - HI - O.

Can you tell me the difference between a fisherman and a dunce?
One baits hooks and the other hates books.

Why are clocks so shy?
Because they always have their hands in front of their faces.

How do you describe pedestrians in Los Angeles?
Los Angeles Dodgers.

What would happen if an eye doctor came into the class-room?
He'd check the pupils.

Why is a river rich?
Because the river has two banks.

Which is heavier—a ton of feathers or a ton of bricks?
Neither; they both weigh two thousand pounds.

What has eighteen legs and catches flies?
A baseball team.

What would the United States be if all the cars were pink?
A pink car-nation.

Kansas, Kalamazoo, and Katonah—how can you spell *them* without a *K?*
T-H-E-M.

What can travel all the way around the world and still stay in one corner?
A postage stamp.

What kind of coat has no buttons and is always put on wet?
A coat of paint.

Why does a duck always look so worried?
Because he always has a bill in front of his face.

What did one eye say to the other?
Just between you and me, there's something that smells.

Why do spiders make good outfielders?
They catch flies.

Did you hear about the fight in the candy store?
Two suckers got licked.

What did the man say to the wall?
One more crack like that and I'll plaster you.

What would happen if you threw a white rock into the
Red Sea?
It would get wet.

What's the best way to catch a squirrel?
Go up a tree and act like a nut.

Have you heard about the magician who walked down
the street and turned into a restaurant?

Why does the ocean roar?
You would, too, if you had lobsters in your bed.

Did you hear the one about the bed?
No.
No wonder, it hasn't been made up yet.

What has keys and can't open locks?
Monkeys, turkeys, and donkeys.

If kings like to sit on their gold, who sits on silver?
The Lone Ranger.

What did the bald man say when he received a comb for
his birthday?
Thanks very much, I'll never part with it.

What is the best way to make a coat last?
Make the vest and trousers first.

When does an automobile go exactly as fast as a train?
When it is on the train.

What has an eye and can't see?
A needle.

What two letters of the alphabet contain nothing?
M. T.

Why is it you find what you are looking for in the last place you look?
You stop looking for it when you find it.

What most resembles half a cheese?
The other half.

It occurs once in every minute, twice in every moment, and yet not once in a billion years. What is it?
The letter *m*.

What is it that we have in December that we don't have in any other month?
The letter *d*.

What driver doesn't have to have a license?
A screw driver.

Where does baby corn come from?
The stalk.

What is a dirty boy crossing the street twice?
A dirty double crosser.

Three men jumped off the George Washington Bridge, and one didn't get his hair wet. How come?
He was bald.

What is the longest word in the world?
Smile—it's a mile between the *s* and the *e*.

When was beef the highest it has ever been?
When the cow jumped over the moon.

Where is the biggest pencil in the world?
Pennsylvania.

Why did the little boy put sun-tan lotion on the chicken?
Because he liked dark meat.

What did one candle say to another?
Are you going out tonight?

Why did the man bring a ladder to the game?
Because the Giants were playing.

A bus driver passed three red lights, four stop signs, and stopped at a fire hydrant. How many tickets did he get?
None, he was walking.

What runs and runs but never gets anywhere?
A clock.

Why do birds fly south?
They can't walk that far.

There were three little girls, and they all went to school under the same umbrella. How come they didn't get wet?
It wasn't raining.

What did one strawberry say to the other strawberry?
If you weren't so fresh, you wouldn't be in this jam.

What did Tarzan say when he saw an elephant coming?
Here comes an elephant.

What is the smallest room in the world?
A mushroom.

What did the tablecloth say to the table?
Stick 'em up. I have you covered.

What is a zebra after it is five years old?
Six years old.

What did one little chimney say to another little chimney?
You're too young to smoke.

What did one tonsil say to the other tonsil?
The doctor is taking me out tonight.

What has twenty heads but can't think?
A book of matches.

What three-word sentence, reading the same backward and forward, did Adam use when he introduced himself to Eve?
Madam, I'm Adam.

On which side does a chicken have the most feathers?
The outside.

When do two and two make more than four?
When they make twenty-two.

What is the difference between here and there?
The letter *t*.

What word is always pronounced wrong?
Wrong.

How many peas in a pint?
One.

If a man gave one son fifteen cents and the other ten cents,
what time would it be?
A quarter to two.

What has no teeth, no mouth, but does have eyes and
lives in the ground?
A potato.

Why did the cowboy die with his boots on?
Because he didn't want to stub his toe when he kicked
the bucket.

What weighs a thousand pounds, has four legs, flies, and is yellow?
Two five-hundred-pound canaries.

Why would a barber rather shave ten men from New York than one from San Francisco?
Because he would get ten times as much money.

What's the biggest diamond in the world?
A baseball diamond.

What did the porcupine say to the cactus plant?
Is that you, Mama?

What's big and red and eats rocks?
A big red rock eater.

What is it that has four legs, eats oats, has a tail, and sees equally well from both ends?
A blind mule.

Give me a sentence using the word "amphibious."
Most fish stories am-fibious.

What did the big hand on the watch say to the little hand?
I'll be around in an hour.

How many balls of string would it take to reach the moon?
Only one if it were long enough.

When the clock strikes thirteen, what time is it?
Time to get it fixed.

Why is a watermelon filled with water?
Because it's planted in the spring.

When is it easy to read in the woods?
When autumn turns the leaves.

What part of an automobile kills the most people?
The nut behind the wheel.

What is found in the very center of America and Australia?
The letter *r*.

What has two thousand eyes and two thousand legs?
One thousand people.

What did one rose say to the other?
Hi, Bud.

How can you change a pumpkin into another vegetable?
Throw it up into the air and it will come down squash.

What kind of pet makes music?
Trum-pet.

What is it you cannot see, yet is always before you?
The future.

What is the happiest letter in the alphabet?
U—because it is always in fun.

What has more lives than a cat?
A frog—it croaks every night.

What is a caterpillar?
An upholstered worm.

What animals have the smallest feet?
The smallest animals.

What did the adding machine say to the clerk?
You can count on me.

Why didn't the baby moth cry when his mother spanked him?
Anyone knows you can't make a moth bawl.

What is larger when cut at both ends?
A ditch.

What is the best thing to keep in winter?
Warm.

Why is a boy like a stream of water?
They both do a lot of running.

What makes a road broad?
The letter *b*.

What is yellow and goes ding-dong?
A yellow ding-dong.

What man always finds things dull?
The scissors sharpener.

What's as round as the moon, as black as paint, and has a hole in the middle?
A record.

What scuffles around all day and sits under the bed at night with its tongue hanging out?
A shoe.

What compares with a dentist's office?
A filling station.

What is a skeleton?
A skeleton is a stack of bones with the people taken off.

What is a twip?
A twip is a wide on a twain.

What word starts with *e* and has only one letter in it?
Envelope.

What did the picture say to the wall?
First they frame me, then they hang me.

If a man were born in Turkey, raised in Italy, came to America, and died in Chicago, what is he?
Dead.

What did the big firecracker say to the little firecracker?
My pop is bigger than your pop.

What is the difference between the North Pole and the South Pole?
All the difference in the world.

Ten potato chips crossed the George Washington Bridge and seven jumped off. Why didn't the other three?
Because they were Wise potato chips.

On what day of the year do girls talk the least?
The shortest day.

What looks like a cat, walks like a cat, eats like a cat, and is not?
A kitten.

How do you spell fish in three letters.
C-o-d.

Why is a mousetrap like the measles?
Both are catching.

What fruits are most often mentioned in history?
Dates.

If you had sixteen cows and two goats, what would you have?
Plenty of milk.

If you drop a letter in the mud, what will you have?
Blackmail.

How do you make a Venetian blind?
Stick a finger in his eye.

What three letters make a sheep of a lamb?
A-g-e.

What did one monocle say to the other monocle?
Let's get together and make spectacles of ourselves!

What can pass before the sun without making a shadow?
The wind.

What goes "99-thump, 99-thump, 99-thump"?
A centipede with a wooden leg.

The Little Joker

BOY JOKER: Are you unattached?
GIRL JOKER: No, I'm just put together sloppily.

FIRST JOKER: Where were you born?
SECOND: In a hospital.
FIRST: No kidding, what was the matter with you?

DOCTOR: Ask the accident victim his name so we can notify his family.
NURSE: He says his family knows his name.

Could this letter be for you? The name's obliterated.
Sorry, my name's Brown.

PSYCHIATRIST QUESTIONING A PATIENT: What would you say would be the difference between a little boy and a dwarf?
PATIENT: Well, there might be a lot of difference.
DOCTOR: What, for instance?
PATIENT: The dwarf might be a girl.

My girl friend has a twin.
How do you tell them apart?
Her brother is taller.

ROBBER: This is a hold-up. Give me your money, or else.
VICTIM: Or else what?
ROBBER: Don't confuse me. This is my first job.

I forgot my mittens.
Why don't you tie a string around your finger?
Okay, but wouldn't the mittens be warmer?

WORKER: Didn't I tell you to notice when the glue boiled over?
HELPER: I did, it was quarter past ten.

PASSENGER: Is this my train?
CONDUCTOR: No sir, it belongs to the railroad company.
PASSENGER: Don't be funny. Can I take this train to New York?
CONDUCTOR: No sir, it's much too heavy.

STRANGER: Look at that bunch of cows.
COWBOY: Not bunch, herd.
STRANGER: Heard what?
COWBOY: Of cows.
STRANGER: Sure, I've heard of cows.
COWBOY: No, I mean a cow herd.
STRANGER: What do I care? I have no secrets from them.

Where are we eating?
Let's eat up the street.
Let's not, I hate concrete.

MOTHER: Who was that calling?
SON: Some lady on the phone said, "It's a long distance from London," and I said, "It sure is."

Gee, I'm glad I wasn't born in France.
Why?
Because I can't speak a word of French.

COWBOY: Hey, you're putting the saddle on backwards.
NEWCOMER: That's all you know about it, you don't even know which way I'm going.

They asked me to work at the Eagle laundry, but I said no.
Why?
I don't know anything about washing eagles.

Did you like the second act of the play?
I didn't see it. The program said, "Second Act, two years later"—and I couldn't wait.

Why did the joker lock his father in the refrigerator?
Because he wanted cold pop.

CUSTOMER: Waiter, I'm in a hurry. Will the griddlecakes be long?
WAITER: No sir, round.

What did the tie say to the coat?
You go on and I'll hang around.

CUSTOMER: Hey, there's an insect in the bottom of my cup.
MANAGER: Listen Bud, if you want your fortune told, go to a gypsy.

A bank had been robbed and the police asked if all the exits had been guarded.
"Yes," said the watchman, "but they must have gone out the entrance."

Why did the joker bring a double-barrel shotgun to the ballgame?
Because the Lions and Tigers were playing.

FIRST JOKER: Where are the things I left cooking on the stove?

SECOND JOKER: Well, the meat caught fire, and I had to use the soup to put it out.

PATIENT: My family thinks there is something wrong with me because I like pancakes.

DOCTOR: There's nothing wrong with that. I like them myself.

PATIENT: Oh, do you? You must come to see me. I have seven trunks full.

Famous last words of well-known jokers—

"Give me a match, I think my gas tank is empty."

"You can take it easy, that train isn't coming fast."

"Step on her, boy, we're only doing seventy-five."

JOKER: I'm sure my vegetable garden will be a success this year.

NEIGHBOR: How can you tell so soon?

JOKER: The chickens have tasted everything, and they're most enthusiastic.

Why did the joker take a ruler to bed with him?
Because he wanted to measure how long he slept.

There was a cowboy who had two horses, but he couldn't tell them apart. He cut off one horse's mane, but it grew back; he cut off the tail, but that grew back, too. A friend suggested that he measure the horses. The cowboy measured them and went to his friend and said, "That was a good idea; the black one was three inches taller than the white one."

FRIEND: Did you take a shower?
JOKER: No, is there one missing?

MRS. DAVIS: Myrtle, this salad tastes terrible. Did you wash the lettuce?
MYRTLE: Yes, ma'am, and used some soapsuds, too.

FARMER: Why are you jumping up and down on the potato patch?
DOPEY: I'm trying to raise mashed potatoes.

Does your umbrella leak like this all the time?
No, only when it rains.

Why did the joker tiptoe past the medicine cabinet?
Because he didn't want to wake the sleeping pills.

The head man found a boy in the stockroom just standing, leaning against a packing case. He asked, "How much are you getting a week?"

The boy answered, "Fifteen dollars."

"Here's your fifteen dollars, now get out of here and don't come back," the boss said angrily. The boy pocketed the money and left. The boss turned to the stockroom manager and demanded, "How long has that fellow been working here?"

"He doesn't work here, he just delivered a package," answered the manager.

A joker visiting the city for the first time came upon a sign which read, Smith Manufacturing Company.

Well, he said, I always knew a lot of Smiths, but I never knew where they came from.

IMPATIENT HUNTER: Why didn't you shoot that tiger?
SECOND HUNTER: Well, I didn't feel that he had the right expression for a rug.

SAILOR: I was shipwrecked and lived on a can of sardines for a week.
JOKER: My, weren't you afraid that you'd fall off?

Why did the little joker drive off the cliff?
To try out his air brakes.

Two jokers were walking along a country road. One of them noticed a man's leg. He said, "I think it's Joe's leg." Next he saw an arm. "Yeah, it's Joe's arm." Next Joe's body, and finally Joe's head. The first joker picked up the head and started shaking it, saying, "Hey, Joe," in a worried tone, "hey, Joe, are you hurt?"

AUNTIE: Aren't ants funny little things? They work and work and never play.
LITTLE JOKER: I don't think so. Every time I go on a picnic, they're all there.

The little joker had just come back from his first football game. A friend asked him: How did you like it?

He answered: Terrible. They were all lined up and ready to play when some smart aleck came up, kicked the ball, and then they all fought over it the rest of the afternoon.

LADY JOKER: I don't want the same kind of flour you sold me last week.
GROCER: What was the matter with it?
LADY JOKER: It was so tough my husband couldn't eat the biscuits I made with it.

COUSIN: What are you doing with a pencil and paper?
JOKER: I'm writing a letter to my brother.
COUSIN: Who're you kidding? You know you don't know how to write.
JOKER: Sure, but my brother doesn't know how to read.

Mr. Smith went to meet his friend at the station. When the friend got off the train, Smith noticed that he was looking rather pale.

"You look sick," he said, "what's wrong?"

"I always get sick when I ride backwards on a train," he answered.

"Why didn't you ask the man across from you to change seats?" asked Mr. Smith.

"I thought of it, but there wasn't anyone there," the friend answered.

I've lost my dog.
Why don't you put an ad in the paper?
There's no sense to that—my dog can't read.

Two jokers shingling a roof:
FIRST JOKER: Why do you keep throwing nails away?
SECOND JOKER: The heads are on the wrong end.
FIRST JOKER: Don't be stupid, save those for the other side.

Housewife in dressing gown and curlers in hair hurries as she hears the garbage man.

HOUSEWIFE: Am I too late for the garbage?

GARBAGE MAN: No, jump right in.

Why don't you take the bus home?
My mother would make me give it back.

Why don't you buy Christmas Seals?
I don't know how to feed them.

ENGLISH STUDENT: Do you like Kipling?
JOKER: I don't know, I've never kippled.

Name a vegetable that begins with Q.
JOKER: Cucumber.

JOKER: I'm glad they named me Billy.
FRIEND: Why?
JOKER: Because that's what everybody calls me.

Why didn't the joker go through the screen door?
He didn't want to strain himself.

Why did the joker take hay to bed?
He wanted to feed his nightmare.

BOY: How can I hit this nail without hitting my fingers?
JOKER: Well, you might try holding the hammer with both hands.

How did the little joker get off the top of a building if he only had a fifty-cent piece and a pocketknife?

Easy, he cut the eagle out of the fifty cents and flew down.

Why did the joker put corn in his shoes?
Because of his pigeon toes.

POSTMAN: I think you've put too much postage on that letter.
JOKER: Oh, dear, I hope it won't go too far.

Why did the joker wear glasses to bed?
Because he thought he might need two drinks of water.

STUDENT: I got bawled out because I didn't know where the Atlantic Ocean was.
JOKER: Remember where you put things.

Whoppers and Insults

A pigeon came home late for dinner one evening with his feathers bedraggled and his eyes bloodshot. He explained, "I was out minding my own business when, bingo, I got caught in a badminton game."

South Dakota is noted for very sudden changes of temperature. One summer day it got so hot that a field of popcorn started popping and really caused a flurry. The cows in the next field thought it was snowing and froze to death watching.

One year at the Liar's Club meeting where everybody told their biggest whopper, the prize was won by a member who merely said, "I never told a lie."

LANDOWNER: What are you doing up that tree, young man?

BOY: One of your apples fell down and I'm trying to put it back.

Once there were three turtles. One day they decided to go on a picnic. When they got there, they realized they had forgotten the soda. The youngest turtle said he would go home and get it if they wouldn't eat the sandwiches until he got back. A week went by, then a month, finally a year, when the two turtles said, "Oh, come on, let's eat the sandwiches."

Suddenly the little turtle popped up from behind a rock and said, "If you do, I won't go."

Some city boys were hiking in the country. One of them came upon a pile of empty milk bottles and yelled excitedly to his friends, "Come quick. I've found a cow's nest."

DINER: Do you serve crabs here?

WAITER: We serve anyone, sit right down.

In a small town the sheriff is also a veterinary. One night the phone rang, and his wife asked the caller, "Do you want the doctor or the sheriff?"

"Both," came the answer, "I can't get my dog to open his mouth and there's a burglar in it."

A missionary was walking down a jungle path in the depths of Africa when he saw a lion coming toward him. He got down on his knees and bowed his head in prayer. When he finished, he looked up and saw the lion doing the same thing. The lion looked up at him and said, "I don't know what you're doing, but I'm saying grace."

A Texas millionaire walked into an automobile showroom. "My wife's sick, what do you have in the way of a get-well car?"

LEADER OF THE GANG: I'll give you to understand that my father is a big man. He's a Lion, a Moose, and an Elk.

ONE OF THE GANG: Gee, how much does it cost to see him?

TRAFFIC COP: Lady, you were doing seventy-five miles an hour.

LADY DRIVER: Oh, isn't that wonderful, and I only learned to drive yesterday!

FRIEND: How did you win all those medals?

SOLDIER: I saved the lives of my outfit.

FRIEND: That's wonderful! How did you do that?

SOLDIER: I shot the cook.

CURIOUS CHARACTER: How did you capture all those elephants?

TIRED HUNTER: When I got to Africa, I took out a blackboard and wrote the word "elephant," but I made sure to spell it wrong. When all the elephants came out to see it spelled incorrectly, I looked at them through the wrong end of my telescope. That made them so small, I picked them up with my tweezers and put them in a bottle.

FISHERMAN: I caught a fish so big that my friends wouldn't let me pull it aboard for fear of swamping the boat.

FRIEND: That reminds me of the same thing that happened to me when I was on the *Queen Mary*.

TOM: Last night I met a girl and fell in love at first sight.

DICK: Why don't you invite her to the dance?

TOM: I took a second look.

A nervous old lady was walking gingerly through a rough part of town. Rain started to fall, and she dodged from one entrance to another. At one of her stops she was startled by a voice saying, "Keep moving lady, I've got you covered." Shaking in her boots, she looked back. There stood a kindly old gentleman holding a big umbrella.

BIG BOY: On my right hand was a lion, on my left was a tiger, in front and in back of me were wild elephants.
LITTLE BOY: What happened?
BIG BOY: The merry-go-round stopped.

NEIGHBOR: I heard you were moving your piano, so I came over to help.
PIANIST: Thanks, it's upstairs already.
NEIGHBOR: Do it alone?
PIANIST: No, I hitched the cat to it.
NEIGHBOR: How could a cat pull a heavy piano like that up a flight of stairs?
PIANIST: Used a whip.

DOCTOR: I don't like the looks of your husband.
WIFE: I don't either, but he is good to the children.

A farmer grew a crop of flax and had a tablecloth made from it. He told a friend about it. The friend obviously didn't believe him, but asked how he did it. The farmer answered, "It was easy, I just planted a napkin."

A singer was practicing enthusiastically when the telephone rang.

VOICE: Say, lady, what's the name of that song you're trying to sing?

SINGER: Why, that's "The Road to Mandalay."

VOICE: For heavens sake, take the detours over those rough spots.

ART CRITIC: When I look at one of your paintings, I stand and wonder——

ARTIST: How I do it?

CRITIC: No, *why* you do it!

When William Howard Taft was campaigning in unfriendly territory, someone threw a cabbage at him as he stood on the platform. It rolled to a stop at his feet. "I see," he said, "that one of my opponents has lost his head."

ALICE: My boy friend has been telling everybody he's going to marry the most beautiful girl in the world.

MARIE: Oh, what a shame. And after all the time you two have been going together.

CUSTOMER: What kind of pie is this supposed to be, apple or peach?

WAITRESS: What does it taste like?

CUSTOMER: Glue.

WAITRESS: Then it's apple. The peach tastes like putty.

BOY: May I hold your hand?
GIRL: It isn't very heavy. I can manage, thank you.

MEDICAL STUDENT: Don't you have any recent books on anatomy? These are all at least fifteen years old.
LIBRARIAN: Young man, there haven't been any new bones added to the human body in that time.

JANE: You'd be a fine dancer except for two things.
JOE: What's that?
JANE: Your feet.

A mother with four young children had to drive them to school several days in a row because they missed the school bus. After enough of this, she dropped them off at the school and said, "Now look here, from now on this coach is turning into a pumpkin."

As the door closed, she heard the youngest say, "Humph, that fairy godmother has sure flipped her lid."

FARMER BOY: Aren't you afraid the birds will eat these seeds? You need a scarecrow.

FARMER GIRL: Oh no, there's always one of us in the garden.

Your teeth are like stars.
They come out at night.

Want to lose ten pounds of ugly fat?
Sure.
Cut off your head.

WIFE: I can hardly believe that such beautiful furs can come from such a small sneaking beast.

HUSBAND: I don't ask for thanks, but the least you can do is show respect.

PATIENT: Give it to me, Doc, how am I?

DOCTOR: Well, if you feel as bad as you look, you've come too late.

JOE: I've got an idea!

JIM: Beginner's luck.

TOURIST: What's your speed limit in this hick town?

LOCAL YOKEL: Haven't got one. You strangers can't go through too fast for us.

The customer had been waiting a long time for his dinner. Finally the waiter appeared and said with a flourish: "Your fish will be ready in a minute or two, sir."

The man looked interested and asked, "What bait are you using?"

SHOE-SHINE BOY: Shine your shoes, Mister?
BUSINESSMAN: No.
SHOE-SHINE BOY: Shine 'em so you can see your face?
BUSINESSMAN: No!
SHOE-SHINE BOY: Don't blame you.

CUSTOMER: This restaurant must have a very clean kitchen.
MANAGER: Thank you, sir, but how did you know?
CUSTOMER: Everything tastes of soap.

MARY: Do you think that Jack would be happy with a girl like me?
ANN: Maybe, if she wasn't *too* much like you.

MRS. SMITH: Whenever I'm in the dumps, I get a new hat.
MRS. JONES: Oh, so that's where you get them.

Puns

SMART ALECK: I was so bright, my father called me *sun* . . .

DINER: Chef, this soup is spoiled.
CHEF: Who told you?
DINER: A little swallow.

How much is five Q and five Q?
Ten Q.
You're welcome.

Did you hear about the big fire at the shoe factory?
Four thousand soles were lost.

Why does it take the runner longer to go from second to
third than from first to second?
Because there's a shortstop in between.

ONE HORSE TO ANOTHER: I don't remember your mane,
    but your pace is familiar.

A minister wanted to telephone another minister in a far-
away city.
The operator asked, "Station to station?"
"No, parson to parson," answered the minister.

How can you tell that dog is young?
Because of his short pants.

How did you get that black eye?
I got hit by a guided muscle.

Your car is at the door.
Yes, I can hear it knocking.

When is an operation funny?
When it leaves the patient in stitches.

A gentleman standing in front of an exhibition of poor art talent labeled Art Objects said to the attendant, "I should think Art would object, and I can't say that I blame him."

What did the rug say to the floor?
Stay where you are, I've got you covered.

YOUNG MAN (to friend riding horseback): Shall we take the bridle path?
COY GIRL: Oh, Harry, this is so sudden.

Have you ever seen a man-eating shark?
No, but I've seen a man eating cod.

FRIEND: Did you learn how to walk a tightrope by yourself?
CIRCUS PERFORMER: No, it has to be taut.

What did the doughnut say to the cake?
If I had as much dough as you have, I wouldn't be hanging around this hole.

A man went to the rocket station and asked for a ticket to the moon.
"Sorry, sir," the attendant said, "the moon is full just now."

Famous punster boasted at a banquet that he could make a pun on any subject.

"Her majesty the Queen," someone said.

Without hesitating, the punster replied, "The Queen is not a subject."

JUDGE: Did you steal this woman's rug?
PRISONER: No, your honor, she gave it to me and told me to beat it.

What do you have if there are two ducks and a cow?
Quackers and milk.

A rabbit and a duck went to a show that cost a dollar. Which one got in?
The duck because he had a bill.

Why is it a mistake to gossip in a stable?
Because all horses carry tails.

SON: Dad, what are those holes in the board for?
DAD: Those are knotholes.
SON: Well, if they're not holes, what are they?

Did you hear about the fish who had the measles?
He just had them on a small scale.

FIRST MOSQUITO: Why are you making such a fuss?
SECOND MOSQUITO: Hurray, I passed the screen test.

HOUSEWIFE: The sausages you sent to me were meat at
one end and bread crumbs at the other.
BUTCHER: I know, but in these times it's impossible to
make both ends meat.

Why does a chicken cross the road?
For fowl purposes.

What is the Mexican weather report?
Chile today, hot tamale.

Do you know what the man got who invented Metrecal?
The no-belly prize.

Why did the old woman put wheels on her rocking chair?
Because she wanted to rock and roll.

Why is it that you can't starve in the Sahara Desert?
Because of all the sand-wich-is there.

WIFE (ordering a new hat): What kind of bird shall I
have on it?
HUSBAND: One with a small bill.

How do you get down off an elephant?
How?
You don't get down off an elephant, you get down off a
duck.

Did you hear the story about the peacock?
It's a beautiful tale.

Did you ever stand on a pet?
No.
I have, on a car-pet.

What's the idea, driving your sheep over my frozen pond?
Aw, I'm only pulling the wool over your ice.

What would you have if your lawn mower ran over a bird?
Shredded tweet.

If you had three ducks and put them in a crate, what would you have?
A box of quackers.

There was a nickel and a dime on top of a big building. The nickel jumped off. Why didn't the dime?

The dime had more sense.

Why shouldn't a doctor be seasick?
Because he is accustomed to see sickness.

Why does an Indian wear feathers?
To keep his wig-wam.

JUDGE TO DENTIST: Do you swear to pull the tooth, the whole tooth, and nothing but the tooth?

What's the difference between unlawful and illegal?
Ill-eagle is a sick bird.

ENGLISHMAN: Your sky here looks much clearer than in London.
CAB DRIVER: Sure! We have more skyscrapers here.

Do you know why Santa Claus planted a garden?
So he can ho, ho, ho.

Why doesn't a bike stand up by itself?
Because it's two-tired.

What is the best day to fry?
Friday.

When one tree is talking to another tree, and another tree
is listening, what is it called?
Leavesdropping.

What is a bull doing in the pasture when he's standing
with his eyes closed?
Bull-dozin'.

Alfie and Archie

ALFIE: The only difference between you and the mule is that the mule wears a collar.
ARCHIE: But I wear a collar, too.
ALFIE: Then I was mistaken—there's no difference.

ALFIE: What's the matter with your thumb?
ARCHIE: I hit the wrong nail.

ARCHIE: Let's play house.
ALFIE: O.K., you be the door and I'll slam you.

ALFIE: Did you fill in that blank yet?
ARCHIE: What blank?
ALFIE: The one between your ears.

ALFIE: Did you know Santa had only seven reindeer last year?

ARCHIE: How come?

ALFIE: Comet went down the drain.

ARCHIE: I can swim with my head above the water.

ALFIE: So what? Wood floats.

ARCHIE: That's a queer pair of socks you have on. One is red and the other's green.

ALFIE: Yes, but the funny thing is that I have another pair at home like these.

ALFIE: Why don't you mend the roof?

ARCHIE: I can't today, it's pouring rain.

ALFIE: Well, why don't you mend it in dry weather?

ARCHIE: It doesn't leak then.

ARCHIE: My grandpa made a scarecrow so terrible that it frightened every single crow off the place.

ALFIE: You think that's something, mine made one that scared 'em so much they brought back the corn they stole last year.

ALFIE: I saw a baby that gained ten pounds in two weeks by drinking elephant's milk.

ARCHIE: You don't say. Whose baby was it?

ALFIE: The elephant's.

ARCHIE: She must be very musical.
ALFIE: How can you tell?
ARCHIE: By the cords in her neck.

ALFIE: I can climb *anything!*
ARCHIE (throwing a flashlight beam upward): I'll bet you can't climb that.
ALFIE: I could, but it would be just like you to turn it off when I was twenty-five feet up, and then where would I be?

ALFIE: People should call you Amazon.
ARCHIE: Why?
ALFIE: Because you're so wide at the mouth.

ARCHIE: Hey, why are you wearing my raincoat?
ALFIE: You wouldn't want your best suit to get wet, would you?

ALFIE: What time do you get up in the morning?
ARCHIE: As soon as the first ray of sun comes into my room.
ALFIE: Isn't that rather early?
ARCHIE: No, my room faces west.

ARCHIE: When you saw that woman driving toward you, why didn't you give her half the road?
ALFIE: I couldn't tell which half she wanted.

ARCHIE: Have you heard about the man who sat up all night trying to figure out where the sun went when it set?

ALFIE: No, what happened?

ARCHIE: It finally dawned on him.

ALFIE: Can you draw a straight line with a ruler?

ARCHIE: Sure.

ALFIE: That's funny, I have to use a pencil.

ARCHIE: I saw something last night I'll never get over.

ALFIE: What was that?

ARCHIE: The moon.

ALFIE: I do my hardest work before breakfast.

ARCHIE: What's that?

ALFIE: Getting up.

ARCHIE: Which hand do you stir your coffee with?

ALFIE: My right, of course.

ARCHIE: I use a spoon.

ARCHIE: There are two things that I simply won't eat for breakfast.
ALFIE: What are they?
ARCHIE: Lunch and dinner.

ALFIE: My father has George Washington's watch in his collection.
ARCHIE: That's nothing. My father has Adam's apple in his.

ALFIE: I'm disgusted.
ARCHIE: Why?
ALFIE: I just stepped on a weighing machine and it said, "One person at a time."

ARCHIE: Did you know I don't have all my toes on one foot?
ALFIE: No, how did it happen?
ARCHIE: I have five on one foot and five on the other.

ARCHIE: Don't bother me, I'm writing to my girl.
ALFIE: But why are you writing so slowly?
ARCHIE: She can't read fast.

ALFIE: What kind of dog is that?
ARCHIE: A police dog.
ALFIE: He sure doesn't look like one.
ARCHIE: Of course not, he's in the secret service.

ARCHIE: Haven't I seen your face before somewhere else?

ALFIE: I don't think so. It's always been right here between my ears.

ALFIE: I have a job in a watch factory.

ARCHIE: What do you do?

ALFIE: Just stand around and make faces.

ALFIE: My little brother just fell into a manhole, what
shall I do?

ARCHIE: Run to the library and get a book on how to
bring up a child.

ARCHIE: What would you do if you were in my shoes?

ALFIE: Polish them.

ARCHIE: May I borrow your blue suit?

ALFIE: Why so formal all of a sudden?

ARCHIE: You've hidden it in a new place.

ALFIE: If I saw a man beating a donkey and stopped him,
what virtue would I be showing?

ARCHIE: Brotherly love.

ALFIE: I just met a big bear.

ARCHIE: Did you give him both barrels?

ALFIE: Both barrels? I gave him the whole gun.

ALFIE: If a butcher was six feet tall and wore size twelve shoes, what would he weigh?
ARCHIE: Meat, stupid.

ARCHIE: Will you give me a dime for a sandwich?
ALFIE: First let me see your sandwich.

ALFIE: You've been working in that garden for hours. What are you growing?
ARCHIE: Tired!

ARCHIE: I bet I could beat a race horse if you'd let me choose the place to run.
ALFIE: Where would you like to run?
ARCHIE: Up a ladder.

ALFIE: What's the difference between a cabbage and a lemon?
ARCHIE: I don't know.
ALFIE: You'd be a fine one to send after lemons.

ARCHIE: Golly, I'm hungry!
ALFIE: What did you have for dinner?
ARCHIE: Company.

ARCHIE: What is the definition of an alarm clock?
ALFIE: Something to scare the daylights into you.

ARCHIE: Do you know how long cows should be milked?
ALFIE: The same as short ones.

ARCHIE: What do you mean the moon's gone broke?
ALFIE: I read in the paper that it's down to its last quarter.

ARCHIE: I lost my sweater.
ALFIE: You can wear mine.
ARCHIE: Then what will you wear?
ALFIE: I'll wear yours.

ARCHIE: You told me to rub grease on my chest to grow tall like you. It didn't work.
ALFIE: What did you use?
ARCHIE: Crisco.
ALFIE: Stupid, that's shortening.

ARCHIE: I've discovered how to improve the taste of salt
ALFIE: How?
ARCHIE: Sprinkle it lightly over hamburger.

ALFIE: Go see if the chef has pig's feet.
ARCHIE: I can't tell. He's got his shoes on.

ARCHIE: Is the refrigerator running?
ALFIE: Yes, it is.
ARCHIE: You had better catch it before it gets away.

ALFIE: I fell over twenty feet last night.
ARCHIE: How come you didn't get hurt?
ALFIE: I was just trying to get to my seat in the movies.

ALFIE: Who gave you the black eye?
ARCHIE: Nobody, I had to fight for it.

STRANGER: Hey, why are you running so fast?
ALFIE: I'm trying to stop two guys from fighting.
STRANGER: Who are they?
ALFIE: Archie and me.

Family Style

DAD: There's something wrong with my shaving brush.
SON: That's funny. It was all right when I painted my bike.

BUS PASSENGER (angrily): Madam, please control your child! He just tore off my wig.
MOTHER: Thank goodness! I thought he scalped you.

MOTHER: What did your father say when he fell off the ladder?
CHILD: Should I leave out the bad words?
MOTHER: Certainly.
CHILD: Nothing.

FATHER: When I was your age, I thought nothing of walking miles to school.
SON: Yeah, Dad, I don't think much of it myself.

SON: Pop, I fell into the crook.
POP: What! With your new suit on?
SON: Yes, Pop, I didn't have time to take it off.

After telling a lie, Billy's father said to him, "If you tell one more lie, I'll use my belt on you."
BILLY: You'd better not, Dad.
FATHER: Why not?
BILLY: Your pants will fall.

WIFE: Oh, stop the car quick! I forgot to turn off the electric iron.
HUSBAND: It's all right, dear, nothing will burn. I forgot to turn off the shower.

LITTLE GIRL TO FATHER: You know, Dad, when Jack Kennedy was your age, he was President.
FATHER: Yes, and when Shirley Temple was your age, she was a millionaire.

SON: Good news, Dad.
DAD: What do you mean?
SON: You won't have to buy me any new books next year. I'm taking all of this year's work over again.

BROTHER: Want to see something swell?

SISTER: Sure!

BROTHER: Hit your head with a baseball bat.

OLDER SISTER: My little sister started walking when she was ten months old.

FRIEND: How old is she now?

OLDER SISTER: Three years.

FRIEND: She must be pretty tired.

DOCTOR: Don't forget I made eight house calls when your son had the chicken pox.

MOTHER: And don't you forget, he infected the whole school for you.

SONNY: It's a good thing that it was adults who split the atom.

FATHER: Why?

SONNY: Well, if one of us kids did it, we'd be told to put it back together.

PAT: What's the best way to teach a girl to swim?

MIKE: First you put your arm around her waist, then——

PAT: She's my sister.

MIKE: Oh, push her off the dock.

DOCTOR: That pain in your left leg is caused by old age.
GRANDMA: Nonsense! My right leg is the same age and it
doesn't hurt a bit.

"Oh, Captain," said a lady on cruise, "my husband is
subject to seasickness. Could you suggest what he should
do in case of an attack?"

"Don't worry, madam," replied the captain, "he'll do it."

Mother, boarding a plane with her daughter, said to the
pilot: "Now don't start going faster than sound, we want
to talk."

DAD AT CHRISTMASTIME: "November runs into December . . .
December runs into Christmas . . .
And Christmas runs into
money."

TOMMY: Come quick, officer, there's a man been fighting
my father for half an hour.
POLICEMAN: Why didn't you tell me before?
TOMMY: 'Cause my father was getting the best of it until
a minute ago.

MOTHER: Dennis, use toothpaste on your toothbrush.
DENNIS: Why? My teeth aren't loose.

NEIGHBOR: How do you tell your twin boys apart?
MOTHER: I pinch them. Dave yells in high *C*, and Pete yells a full tone lower.

BOY: Will you marry me?
GIRL: Have you seen my father?
BOY: Many times, but I love you just the same.

Mom, I got *F* in arithmetic.
How did that happen?
The girl I copy from was absent.

LITTLE BOY: What was the name of the last station where this train stopped?
MOTHER: I don't remember, why?
LITTLE BOY: Because baby sister got off there.

WIFE: I got the car fixed. Now it starts.
HUSBAND: How much did it cost?
WIFE: Only two dollars.
HUSBAND: What was wrong?
WIFE: It needed gas.

Mike's grandfather told him that he would give him a dime if he would be a good boy all week. At the end of the week the grandfather said, "Have you been a good boy? Do you think you really deserve the dime?"

Mike answered, "Better give me a penny."

MOTHER: Janie, why did you get such a low grade in spelling?

JANIE: I put too many *z*'s in scissors.

SONNY: Daddy, there was a man here today to see you.

DADDY: With a bill?

SONNY: No, just an ordinary nose like yours.

MOTHER: Frankie, why did you kick your little sister in the stomach?

FRANKIE: Couldn't help it, she turned around too quick.

FATHER: How did you get Buddy to take his medicine without a squawk?

MOTHER: I shot it into his mouth from a water pistol.

UNCLE: And what are you going to be when you get through school?

SONNY: An old, old man.

Child psychologist to mother: "You'll have to handle this child carefully. Remember, you're dealing with a sensitive, high-strung little stinker."

LITTLE BOY: Grandpa, were you in the ark?

GRANDPA: No.

LITTLE BOY: Then why didn't you drown?

An insurance man was teaching his wife to drive. Suddenly the brakes failed.

"I can't stop," she cried, "what will I do?"

"Don't panic, just hit something cheap," he said.

MOTHER: Why are you crying?
JIMMY: Daddy hit his hand with a hammer.
MOTHER: You should be laughing.
JIMMY: I did.

FATHER: If you want to find out something, start at the bottom.
CHILD: But I want to learn to swim.

Little Patsy was taken to church for the first time. As she walked out with her parents, the minister asked how she liked church. "I liked the music," she said, "but the commercial was too long."

FATHER: How did the window get broken?
SONNY: I was cleaning my sling-shot and it went off.

AUNT: Did you hear about poor Uncle Herbert being drowned while visiting Italy?
COUSIN: How did it happen?
AUNT: He got into a street fight in Venice.

A child's persistent sniffling annoyed a woman sitting next to him in the movies. Finally she said, "Haven't you got a handkerchief?"

"Yes," replied the child, "but my mother won't let me loan it to anybody."

Father teaching his daughter to drive: "Stop on red, go on green, and take it easy when I turn purple."

A salesman knocked on the screen door of a house and saw a small boy practicing the piano. He asked, "Is your mother home, sonny?"

The boy answered angrily, "What do you think!"

Girl talking to friend about her boy friend who stood her up to go fishing: "If you want to find him, just go down to the bridge and look for a pole with a worm on each end."

Wildlife

MAMA OWL: I'm worried about Baby.
PAPA OWL: Why?
MAMA OWL: He doesn't give a hoot about anything.

A boy was walking with his dog. A policeman came by and asked: "Does that dog have a license?"

The boy answered, "He doesn't need one, he isn't old enough to drive."

When the baby sardine saw a submarine for the first time, his mother said, "Don't be scared, it's just a can of people."

MAN: One mouse trap, please. I have to catch a train.
CLERK: Sorry, sir, our traps aren't that big.

PAPA KANGAROO: Mama, where's baby?
MAMA KANGAROO: Oh, dear, I think I had my pocket
picked.

Once upon a time a man and his wife were touring
Russia. Their guide's name was Rudolph, and the husband
and Rudolph argued all the time. As the couple was leav-
ing Moscow, the husband said, "Look, it's snowing out."

The guide argued, "No, sir, it's raining out."

"I still think it's snowing," said the husband.

Then the wife said, "Rudolph the Red knows rain dear."

One very angry skunk said to another: "So do you!"

CITY DWELLER: Why don't you shoo these mosquitoes?
FARMER: It would cost too much, let them go barefoot.

FISHERMAN: Where are you going with that lobster?
FRIEND: I'm taking him home for dinner.
LOBSTER: I've already had my dinner, take me to a movie.

TOURIST: I don't like all these flies around here.

NATIVE: To be honest, there are some of them I don't care for either.

Hillbilly's wife to druggist: "Now be shore an' write plain on them medicine bottles which is fer the horse an' which is fer my husband. I don't want nothin' to happen to that horse afore spring plowin'."

PAT: It's raining cats and dogs.

MIKE: I know, I just stepped into a poodle.

A salesman sees a huge animal and asks, "What breed is it?"

The old man answered, "I don't know, my nephew sent it to me from Africa."

SALESMAN: Odd-looking dog.

OLD MAN: Lot odder looking before I cut all its mane off!

QUESTION: Why does your dog keep turning around in circles?

ANSWER: He's a watch dog and he's winding himself up.

BABY GROUNDHOG: One of those foreign cars ran over me.

MOTHER GROUNDHOG: You shouldn't be playing out in the street.

BABY GROUNDHOG: I wasn't—it came down the hole after me.

GUIDE: A tiger will not harm you if you carry a white walking stick.

HUNTER: Yes, but how fast must you carry it?

Hunter after shooting at a duck: "You're seeing a miracle—there goes a flying dead duck!"

A little boy was asked what animal he would like to be. "A lion," he answered, "so's I could eat up our landlady."

A man riding a horse passed a dog on the road.

"Good morning," said the dog.

"I didn't know dogs could talk," said the man.

"Neither did I," said the horse.

Jim dropped in on Tom and was surprised to find him playing chess with his dog.

JIM: That's the most amazing dog I've ever seen.

TOM: Oh, he isn't so smart, I beat him three games out of four.

MOTHER LION: Junior, what are you doing?

BABY LION: I'm chasing a hunter around a tree.

MOTHER LION: Junior, how often have I told you not to
play with your food!

DRIVER: I had to run into the fence to keep from hitting
a cow.

FRIEND: Was it a Jersey cow?

DRIVER: I didn't see its license.

Sign Language

In the age of rock 'n roll, a sign in a drugstore read: "Teen-age spoken here."

Sign in the showroom of a foreign-car dealer reads: We give demonstration rides in your living room.

Once there was an elevator operator who got tired of people asking him for the right time. He hung a clock in his elevator. Now all day long people ask him, "Is that clock right?"

SIGN ON A BAKERY TRUCK: Pass the bread, please.

Sɪɢɴ ᴏɴ Vᴇɢᴇᴛᴀʙʟᴇ Tʀᴜᴄᴋ: Squash, do not crush.

Sign in a factory:
  Whistle while you work, it'll drive everyone batty.

Found within a small boy's book: I pity the brook
                                  I pity the stream
                                  I pity the crook
                                  Who steals this book.

A sign seen over a desk: The human brain is wonderful.
It starts working the minute you wake up and never stops
until you're called on in class.

Sign in an antique store:
  Come in and buy what your grandmother threw out.

VISITOR IN NEWSPAPER OFFICE: Where is the editor's office, please?

BOY: Go up the stairway marked NO ADMITTANCE, and walk through the door marked KEEP OUT. Walk straight ahead until you get to the sign marked SILENCE, and then yell for him.

Sign over an awning store:
Come in for a shady deal.

Sign in a funeral parlor window:
We give Green Stamps.

Sign in a restaurant:
Eat now, pay waiter.

Street sign: To avoid that run-down feeling, look both ways before crossing the street.

Sign in a restaurant: Don't laugh at our coffee. You too, may be old and weak someday.

SCHOOL SIGN: Laugh and the class laughs with you; but you stay after school alone!

Mishmash

Is it bad luck for a black cat to walk behind you?
That depends on whether you are a man or a mouse.

FARMER: I named that pig "Ink."
VISITOR: Why such a strange name?
FARMER: Because he is always running out of the pen.

I hope the rain keeps up.
Why?
So it won't come down.

Did you hear about the girl who was so cross-eyed that
when she cried, the tears from her right eye fell on her
left cheek?

Do you know what happened to the girl who didn't know
the difference between cold cream and putty?
No, what?
All her windows fell out.

DOCTOR: Well, you'll get along O.K. Your left leg is swol-
    len, but I wouldn't worry about it.
PATIENT: No, and if your leg were swollen, I wouldn't
    worry about it either.

You tell 'em mountain—I'm only a bluff.

ACTOR: Why did you quit the stage?
COMEDIAN: Ill health.
ACTOR: What do you mean, ill health?
COMEDIAN: I made people sick.

What goes well with purple, green, pink, and blue striped
socks?
Hip boots.

LITTLE BOY: Baa, baa, black sheep, have you any wool?
BLACK SHEEP: What do you think this is—nylon?

My hair is coming out—what can I get to keep it in?
A paper bag.

LADY TO OFFICER (standing in the middle of the street): Can you tell me how to get to the hospital?

OFFICER: Just stand where you are.

ANGRY DINER: Waiter, I don't like all these flies that are buzzing around my plate.

WAITER: Well, sir, if you'll just point out the ones you don't like, I'll shoo them away.

LADY PATIENT: Doctor, when I get well, will I be able to play the piano?

DOCTOR: Of course.

LADY PATIENT: That's marvelous. I never played it before.

Did you know Johnny beats his brother up every morning? Really?

Yes. He gets up at seven and his brother gets up at eight.

BUM: Do you have any strawberry shortcake or ice cream, ma'am?

LADY: I don't, but how about some bread and butter?

BUM: I don't think so lady—you see, today is my birthday.

FARMER: Quite a storm we had last night.

NEIGHBOR: Yep, sure was.

FARMER: Damage your barn any?

NEIGHBOR: Dunno, haven't found it yet.

My friend used to roll around until he found out squares can't roll.

Seen in local paper: Wanted: female cat for light mouse-keeping.

BOY: Do you know that man over there? He's the meanest man I ever met.
GIRL: Do you know who I am? I'm that man's daughter.
BOY: Do you know who I am?
GIRL: No.
BOY: Thank goodness.

HOLD-UP MAN (pointing a gun at movie cashier): The picture is terrible. Gimme everybody's money back.

An old lady on a bus, afraid she would miss her stop, poked the driver with her umbrella. "Is this the First National Bank?" she asked.

"No," he replied, "those are my ribs."

Are raw oysters healthy?
Well, we've never heard one complain.

An adult is one who has stopped growing except in the middle.

COMPLAINING NEIGHBOR: Your dog comes and eats my garbage every morning.
DOG LOVER: I hope it's good garbage.

LITTLE GIRL: Give us one ticket to the movie, please.
TICKET SELLER: One? But there are two of you.
LITTLE GIRL: I know, but we're half sisters.

Two beatniks were wandering through a museum. They paused to read the inscription on a statue of Julius Caesar.

"Man," said one beatnik, "it says here this cat's been gone for two thousand years."

"Crazy," replied the other. "Those Romans really knew how to live."

The reason a dog has so many friends is that his tail wags instead of his tongue.

PATIENT: Hey, that wasn't the tooth I wanted pulled.
DENTIST: Just be patient, I'm coming to it.

GIRL: Are you fond of moving pictures?

BOY: Oh, yes, very.

GIRL: Then you won't mind moving some down out of the attic for Mother.

There won't be any witches this year.
They're all on strike for electric brooms.

MR. SMITH: I'm thinking of hiring that Jones boy who used to work for you. Is he steady?

MR. YOUNG: Well, if he were much steadier, he'd be motionless.

DOCTOR: How is the boy who swallowed the half-dollar?

NURSE: No change yet, sir.

BOY: Nurse, may I have a banana?

NURSE: No dear, a banana would be much too heavy for you to eat.

BOY: But wouldn't you hold it for me while I eat it?

Are you chewing gum?
No, I'm Abe Smith.

OLD LADY: Shall I take this train to Chicago?

CONDUCTOR: No thanks, the engineer will do that.

CUSTOMER: One thousand pins and needles, please.

SALESMAN: What's all that for?

CUSTOMER: I'm a sword-swallower and I'm on a diet.

SALESLADY: Isn't it a pretty dolly? You can put it to bed and it will close its eyes and go right to sleep, just like a real baby.

LITTLE GIRL: I can see you don't know babies very well.

MOLLY: How did that naughty little brother of yours get hurt?

SALLY: That good little brother of yours hit him with a brick.

LITTLE BOY: How much are haircuts?

BARBER: Fifty cents.

LITTLE BOY: Well, cut a dime's worth off, please.

WIFE: Doctor, my husband limps because his right leg is shorter than his left. What would you do in this case?

DOCTOR: Probably limp.

PATIENT: Are you sure I'll get well? I've heard doctors sometimes give wrong diagnoses, and treat patients for pneumonia who later die of typhoid fever.

DOCTOR: Don't worry, when I treat a man for pneumonia, he dies of pneumonia.

FOURTH-GRADER IN BED WITH A COLD: How high is my
    temperature, Doctor?
DOCTOR: A hundred and three, Buddy.
FOURTH-GRADER: What's the world's record?

This tonic will grow hair on a billiard ball.
Who wants hair on a billiard ball!

PATIENT TO PSYCHIATRIST: Help me, Doctor. I can't
    remember anything for more than a few minutes. It's
    driving me crazy.
PSYCHIATRIST: How long has this been going on?
PATIENT: How long has what been going on?

BARKER: Step right up, folks, and see the white hen lay
    brown eggs.
SPECTATOR: What's so marvelous about that?
BARKER: Well, can you do it?

A woman finding a rabbit inside her refrigerator said,
"What are you doing there?"
The rabbit said, "This is a Westinghouse, isn't it?"
She answered, "Yes."
RABBIT: "I'm just westing."

CUSTOMER: I'd like to try on that skirt in the window.
CLERK: It would be better if you'd use the dressing room.

TELEPHONE VOICE: Weather Bureau?
WEATHER BUREAU: Yes.
VOICE: How are chances for a shower tonight?
WEATHER BUREAU: O.K. by me. Take one if you need it.